Favourite North Indian Recipes

Favourite North Indian Recipes

Vijaylakshmi Baig

Lustre Press
Roli Books

Flavours of North India

Food follows the movement of people. North India has been at the epicentre of so many such movements that it is the melting pot of many culinary traditions. The Tomar Rajputs were the first contributors in the 11th century. Then came the Afghans followed by the Sultanate, Tughlaq, Lodi, Mughal, and British rulers.

As the region developed, arts and cultures refined and fused. Food demonstrates this best. Customary hospitality changed food habits from their rough peasant beginnings to delicate, even decadent levels of sophistication. The *amirs* (noblemen) sought and stole the cooks and their culinary secrets from their rivals.

While the rulers and grandees indulged themselves their tradesmen developed their culinary traditions in their humble neighbourhood. Delhi and Lucknow soon became bastions of culinary extravagance. Chandni Chowk in Delhi had once been a wide shopping arcade with a raised stone channel of water running down the centre. It had been called the *Nehar Bisht* or the Heavenly Canal. But it fell into disrepair at the end of the Mughal period and its water became unfit to drink. So the emperor ordered the royal *hakim* (doctor) to prescribe food that would aid digestion. He prescribed a number of spices consisting of different kinds of salts and chillies, and cumin seeds, coriander seeds, yoghurt, mint leaves, lemon, and tamarind. These were known to keep the stomach cool. Mixed with crisp, fried biscuits (*papri*) it quickly became a delicacy and Delhi's famous *chaat* was born.

Kulfi (old fashioned Indian ice cream) was first made in the area where the potters lived, Kumarbara. It is here that they made the baked, earthen containers for the *kulfis*. There were many types of *kulfis* such as *aam* (mango), *malai* (cream), and *pista* (pistachio). Some were made in containers scooped out of fruits. As there were no refrigerators, *kulfis* were set in earthen containers, sealed and then covered in large, earthen pots filled with *shoora* (a rough salt) and ice. The pot was rotated by hand to retain a smooth consistency. The *kulfi* took about two hours to set.

Most of the silversmiths, shopkeepers, and craftsmen were poor and many were religiously inclined to vegetarian food. They began to evolve typical Jain and Bania food. The parathas are still famous. Other delicacies are *bharvin puri* (black gram-stuffed fried bread), *khasta kachauri* (deep-fried flour puffs), and *phirni* (powdered rice pudding). On Id, *biryani* was made in three tiers with three colours and each layer was generously layered with cream before being layered with lamb.

Between the trading class and the nobles developed a caste of Kayasthas who were well-educated Hindus employed as clerks and advisors to the *amirs* and agents for the considerable trading enterprises conducted by the royal ladies. Their proximity to the Mughal nobles resulted in a very refined food tradition with an inventive mix of vegetarian and meat dishes. Their distinctive *pulaos*, kebabs, and *rogan josh* were different from the rough frontier foods they originally were.

After Independence came a new wave of refugees from Punjab. Their hearty peasant foods merged to offer tandoori chicken, fish, *sarson ka saag* (spicy mustard greens), *makkai ki roti* (maize flour bread), and *gajar halwa* (saffron-flavoured carrot pudding).

Today, international influences are commonly found on the North Indian platter. India's genius for fusion has given the region an unparalleled variety of food and a distinctive flavour all its own.

Basic Preparations

Garam masala: Masalas should be made in small quantities so that they are not kept for too long on the kitchen shelf. Freshly ground masala has a wonderful flavour which diminishes with storing.

Take 10 gm green cardamoms (*choti elaichi*), 10 gm cinnamon (*dalchini*) sticks, 10 gm cloves (*laung*), 6 black cardamoms (*badi elaichi*), 50 gm cumin (*jeera*) seeds, ½ nutmeg (*jaiphal*), 5 gm black cumin seeds (*shah jeera*), and 5-6 blades of mace (*javitri*).

Dry the spices in the sun, then roast and grind them to a fine powder. Store in an airtight bottle.

Chaat masala: Take 1 tbsp / 8 gm roasted cumin (*jeera*) seeds, a pinch of mint powder, ½ tsp ginger powder (*sonth*), ½ tsp red chilli powder, ½ tsp black pepper (*kali mirch*) powder, 3 tbsp mango powder (*amchur*), 1½ tbsp black salt (*kala namak*), and a pinch of asafoetida (*hing*).

Pound the cumin seeds and mix it with the other spices. Sieve and store in ar airtight jar.

Tomato purée: Take 250 gm tomatoes, add ½ cup water. Pressure cook for 10 minutes. Keep aside to cool. When cool, liquidise and strain. Use as required.

Tamarind (*imli*) pulp: Take 200 gm of seedless tamarind. Add 3 cups water and boil for 5 minutes. Strain the mixture and use as required.

Prepared saffron (*kesar*): Soak a pinch of saffron in 1 tbsp water for 10 minutes. Then grind in a mortar and pestal and use as required.

Garlic-ginger (*lasan-adrak*) paste: Take equal amounts of garlic and ginger and soak overnight. Peel, chop and process in an electric blender with small quantity of water. Blend at high speed to make a smooth paste. Remove and store in an airtight container and refrigerate. The paste will keep for up to 4-6 weeks.

Yoghurt (*dahi*): If you want to set yoghurt at home buy starter from any store or sweet shop.

Heat 1 lt of milk till it is warm to touch. Add 2 tsp of yoghurt to it and stir well. Transfer to a clay pot, cover with a lid and then keep in a warm place to allow it to set. In winter, it usually takes longer to set and also needs to be kept warmer than usual. In the summer months, it sets in a relatively shorter time.

Khasta Kachauri
Deep-fried flour puffs

Preparation time: 2½ hrs.
Cooking time: 10 min.
Serves: 8

Ingredients:

Refined flour (*maida*)	2 cups / 200 gm
Salt to taste	
Bicarbonate of soda	a pinch
Ghee	1 tbsp / 15 gm
For the filling:	
Split black gram (*dhuli urad dal*), washed, soaked for 2 hours, drained	1 cup / 150 gm
Cumin (*jeera*) seeds	1 tsp / 2 gm
Asafoetida (*hing*)	a pinch
Coriander (*dhaniya*) powder	2 tsp / 3 gm
Red chilli powder	½ tsp / 1 gm
Salt	1 tsp / 4 gm

Vegetable oil for frying

Method:

1. Sift the flour, salt, and bicarbonate of soda. Rub in the ghee and knead with enough water to make a hard dough. Keep aside for 30 minutes.
2. **For the filling,** grind all the ingredients together coarsely on a stone slab or in a mixer. Sauté the filling in 1 tbsp ghee till golden. Keep aside to cool.
3. Divide the flour dough into 16 balls. Shape each ball into a small cup; fill 1 tbsp filling into the hollow, pinch together to seal and pat into rounds.
4. Heat the oil in a wok (*kadhai*); deep-fry the rounds, a few at a time, on low heat till they puff up and become crisp and golden. Remove and drain the excess oil on absorbent kitchen paper towels.
5. Serve hot with *aloo ki khatti tarkari* (see p. 38).

Kalmi Bare

Fried mixed gram cakes

Preparation time: 4-5 hrs.
Cooking time: 20 min.
Serves: 6

Ingredients:

Bengal gram (*chana dal*), washed, soaked for 4-5 hours, drained	2 cups / 320 gm
Split black gram (*dhuli urad dal*), washed, soaked for 4-5 hours, drained	½ cup / 75 gm
Salt	1 tsp / 4 gm
Black peppercorns (*sabut kali mirch*), freshly ground	12
Ginger (*adrak*), grated	1 tbsp / 24 gm
Green chillies, finely chopped	2-3
Asafoetida (*hing*)	a pinch
Cumin (*jeera*) seeds	1 tbsp / 6 gm
Coriander (*dhaniya*) seeds	2 tbsp / 12 gm
Green coriander (*hara dhaniya*), finely chopped	a bunch
Ghee for frying	

Method:

1. Grind the Bengal gram and black gram separately to a coarse and grainy paste. Now mix the pastes and the remaining ingredients (except ghee).
2. With wet hands, take some paste and make a 3″-large, round cake. Repeat till all the mixture is used up.
3. Heat the ghee in a pan till hot; deep-fry the cakes, a few at a time. When small bubbles appear on the surface, turn and fry the other side till pale golden. Remove and drain the excess oil on absorbent kitchen paper towels. Keep aside to cool.
4. Then cut each cake into ¼″ slices. Reheat the ghee and fry the slices till golden and crisp. Sprinkle some *chaat* masala and serve with *pudina* chutney.

Moong Dal Cheela

Green gram pancakes

Preparation time: 5 hrs.
Cooking time: 20 min.
Serves: 2-4

Ingredients:

Split green gram (*dhuli moong dal*), soaked for 5 hours	1 cup / 190 gm
Cumin (*jeera*) powder	½ tsp
Ginger-chilli paste	1 tsp / 5 gm
Salt to taste	
Ghee for frying	

Method:

1. Drain and grind the split green gram in a mixer or on a stone slab.
2. Add the remaining ingredients (except ghee) and mix well.
3. Heat 2 tsp ghee in a pan; drop in a ladleful of the green gram batter and spread it evenly with the back of a spoon. Sprinkle some ghee around the sides and lift the edges, so that the ghee can slip under. Turn the pancake over, drizzle some more ghee and cook till brown on both sides. Remove and repeat till all the batter is used up.
4. Serve with green chutney or tomato sauce.

Chaat Papri

Flour crispies topped with yoghurt

Preparation time: 30 min.
Cooking time: 15 min.
Serves: 4

Ingredients:

Refined flour (*maida*)	1 cup / 100 gm
Semolina (*suji*)	1 tbsp / 10 gm
Salt	½ tbsp
Baking powder	a pinch
Vegetable oil	¾ cup / 150 ml
Vegetable oil for frying	
To serve:	
Potatoes, boiled, cubed	½ cup
Chickpeas (*kabuli chana*), boiled	½ cup
Tamarind chutney (see p. 79)	¾ cup / 150 gm
Mint chutney (see p. 75)	4 tbsp / 60 gm
Yoghurt (*dahi*), beaten	1 cup / 180 gm
Chaat masala to taste (see p. 6)	

Method:

1. Sift the refined flour, semolina, salt, and baking powder together. Add hot oil and mix well. Knead with enough water to make a smooth dough.
2. Divide the dough equally into tiny balls. Roll each out into a very thin disc, 1½"in diameter. Perforate each with a fork so that it doesn't puff out while frying. Keep aside for 30 minutes, uncovered.
3. Heat the oil in a wok (*kadhai*); deep-fry the discs on a medium flame till crisp and golden. Remove with a slotted spoon and drain the excess oil on absorbent kitchen paper towels.
4. To serve, arrange the fried discs (*papri*) on a plate; spread the potatoes, chickpeas, tamarind and mint chutneys, yoghurt and *chaat* masala to taste.

Shammi Kebab

Melt-in-the-mouth lamb patties

Preparation time: 45 min.
Cooking time: 45 min.
Serves: 4-6

Ingredients:

Lamb, finely minced, without any fat	1 kg
Bengal gram (*chana dal*), soaked for ½ hour	1¼ cups / 200 gm
Cumin (*jeera*) seeds	1 tsp / 2 gm
Ginger (*adrak*), 1″ piece	1
Onion, medium, sliced, browned	1
Coriander (*dhaniya*) seeds, powdered	1 tbsp / 5 gm
Garam masala (see p. 6)	2 tsp / 4 gm
Eggs	2
Green chillies, chopped	4
Green coriander (*hara dhaniya*), chopped	1 tbsp / 4 gm
Salt to taste	
Vegetable oil for frying	
Onion, cut into rings	1
Mint (*pudina*) leaves	10

Method:

1. Add the lamb mince, drained Bengal gram, cumin seeds, ginger, and ½ cup water in a pressure cooker; cook till you hear the first whistle.
2. Turn off the flame, but do not open the cooker till the pressure dies down completely.
3. Now open the cooker, return to heat and cook till the mixture is completely dry. Remove and keep aside to cool.
4. When the mixture is cool enough to handle, add the browned onion and coriander powder. Grind the mixture on a stone slab or in a mixer.

5. Add the eggs, green chillies, green coriander, and salt. Mix well.
6. Divide the paste into 20 portions. Make small, round patties; slightly flatten them between your palms.
7. Refrigerate for 30 minutes before frying, to avoid the patties from breaking while frying.
8. Heat the oil in a wok (*kadhai*); deep-fry the patties, a few at a time, till brown. Remove with a slotted spoon and drain the excess oil on absorbent kitchen paper towels.
9. Serve hot garnished with onion rings and mint leaves.

Note: *When the minced meat has fat in it, the kebabs or koftas will not bind properly. Always add the eggs a little at a time, to avoid getting a sticky paste. Very often one needs less egg than prescribed in the recipe.*

(Photograph on page 2)

Nahari Gosht

Spicy lamb in a thick gravy

Preparation time: 30 min.
Cooking time: 1 hr.
Serves: 6

Ingredients:

Lamb with bones, cut into small pieces	1 kg
Ghee	2 tbsp / 30 gm
Onion, sliced	1
Cinnamon (*dalchini*), 1″ sticks	2
Bay leaves (*tej patta*)	2
Onion, chopped	1
Black cardamoms (*badi elaichi*)	3
Cloves (*laung*)	5
Coriander (*dhaniya*) powder	2 tsp / 3 gm
Red chilli powder	1 tsp / 2 gm
Turmeric (*haldi*) powder	½ tsp / 1 gm
Garlic (*lasan*) paste	2½ tsp / 15 gm
Ginger (*adrak*) paste	2″ piece
Salt to taste	
Yoghurt (*dahi*), beaten	1 cup / 180 gm
Refined flour (*maida*)	1 tsp / 3 gm
Gram flour (*besan*)	2 tsp / 6 gm
Garam masala (see p. 6)	1 tsp / 2 gm
Mace (*javitri*), powdered	½ tsp / 1 gm
Aniseed (*saunf*), powdered	1 tsp / 2 gm
Green cardamoms (*choti elaichi*), powdered	5
Saffron (*kesar*)	a few strands
Lemon (*nimbu*) juice	1 tbsp / 15 ml
Green coriander (*hara dhaniya*)	4 tbsp / 100 gm
Vetiver (*kewda*) essence (optional)	2 tsp / 10 ml

Method:

1. Heat the ghee in a pan; add the sliced onion, cinnamon sticks, and bay leaves; sauté over medium heat until golden brown. Add the lamb,

chopped onion, black cardamoms, and cloves; cook till the liquid has evaporated.

2. Add the coriander powder, red chilli powder, turmeric powder, garlic paste, ginger paste, and salt; sauté until the oil separates.
3. Add the yoghurt and bring the mixture to the boil. Reduce heat to medium and cook for about 15 minutes.
4. Add 2 cups water and bring to the boil again, cover and simmer, stirring occasionally, until the lamb is tender. Remove the lamb from the gravy and keep aside.
5. Heat 1 tbsp ghee in a pan; add the refined flour and gram flour; sauté over low heat, stirring constantly until light brown. Stir in the gravy. Strain the thick gravy through a soup strainer, reheat the gravy and bring to the boil.
6. Add the lamb, *garam* masala, mace powder, aniseed powder, green cardamom powder, saffron, and lemon juice; mix well and cook on low heat for 30 minutes.
7. Vetiver essence is added just before serving, but it is optional.
8. Garnish with green coriander and serve with *tandoori roti* (see p. 60) or *badshahi naan* (see p. 62).

Subz Gosht

Lamb with turnips and spinach

Preparation time: 30 min.
Cooking time: 45 min.
Serves: 6

Ingredients:

Lamb, boneless, cut into cubes	1 kg
Turnips (*shalgam*), cut into cubes	250 gm
Spinach (*palak*), roughly chopped	500 gm
Mustard (*sarson*) oil	¼ cup / 50 ml
Onions, sliced	½ cup / 120 gm
Garlic (*lasan*) paste	3 tbsp / 54 gm
Ginger (*adrak*) paste	3 tbsp / 54 gm
Turmeric (*haldi*) powder	1 tsp / 2 gm
Salt to taste	
Tomatoes, chopped	250 gm
Red chilli powder	1 tsp / 2 gm
Cloves (*laung*)	8
Cinnamon (*dalchini*), 1" stick	1
Green cardamoms (*choti elaichi*)	5
Mace (*javitri*)	5 blades

Method:

1. Heat the mustard oil in a wok (*kadhai*); add the onions and sauté till light brown. Add the lamb, turnips, and spinach. Sauté for a while.
2. Add the garlic paste, ginger paste, and turmeric powder. Sauté for 30 minutes, and mix in the salt.
3. When the lamb is browned, add the tomatoes and red chilli powder. Mix well.
4. Grind the cloves, cinnamon stick, green cardamoms, and mace to a fine powder.
5. When the lamb is half cooked, add the ground spices. Cook on low heat till the mixture is almost dry and the lamb is tender.
6. Serve hot with steamed rice or *rotis*.

Khara Masala Gosht

Lamb cooked with whole spices

Preparation time: 15 min.
Cooking time: 2 hrs.
Serves: 6

Ingredients:

Lamb, cut into pieces	1 kg
Vegetable oil	½ cup / 100 ml
Onions, finely chopped	2
Fennel (*moti saunf*) seeds	1 tsp / 2 gm
Coriander (*dhaniya*) powder	1 tsp / 1½ gm
Cumin (*jeera*) powder	1 tsp / 1½ gm
Cloves (*laung*)	8
Cinnamon (*dalchini*), 2″ stick	1
Green cardamoms (*choti elaichi*)	5
Ginger (*adrak*) paste	1 tbsp / 18 gm
Garlic (*lasan*) paste	1 tbsp / 18 gm
Salt to taste	
Yoghurt (*dahi*)	1½ cups / 250 gm
Garam masala (see p. 6)	½ tsp / 1 gm

Method:

1. Heat the oil in a pan; add the onions, sauté till light brown. Add the whole and powdered spices, lamb, ginger paste, garlic paste, salt, and yoghurt; mix well.
2. Cover with a thick lid that can hold about 1 cm of water on it, and cook on a low flame for 2 hours.
3. Remove the lid and continue to cook if you want the preparation to be dry.
4. Add the *garam* masala, mix well and serve hot.

Note: *This is* dum pukht *style of cooking. The lamb cooks in its own juices and as long as there is water on the lid, the ingredients inside the pan will never burn.*

Badami Gosht Korma

Lamb braised in yoghurt and almond sauce

Preparation time: 15 min.
Cooking time: 1 hr.
Serves: 4

Ingredients:

Lamb, boneless, cut into cubes	500 gm
Vegetable oil	½ cup / 100 ml
Cinnamon (*dalchini*), 1″ sticks	2
Green cardamoms (*choti elaichi*)	3
Cloves (*laung*)	4
Bay leaves (*tej patta*)	6
Ginger (*adrak*) paste	1½ tbsp / 27 gm
Garlic (*lasan*) paste	1½ tbsp / 27 gm
Green chilli paste	1½ tbsp / 27 gm
Yoghurt (*dahi*)	¼ cup / 45 gm
Almond (*badam*) paste	½ cup / 100 gm
Salt	1 tsp / 4 gm
Black pepper (*kali mirch*) powder	¼ tsp
Saffron (*kesar*)	a few strands
Egg, hard-boiled, quartered	1

Method:

1. Heat the oil in a pan; add the cinnamon sticks, green cardamoms, cloves, and bay leaves. Sauté till they turn brown.
2. Add the ginger paste, garlic paste, and green chilli paste. Fry for a few minutes then add the yoghurt and lamb. Mix well. Cover and cook on low heat for 45 minutes or till the lamb is tender.
3. Add the almond paste, salt, black pepper, and saffron; cook for about 5 minutes till well blended. Remove the pan from the heat.
4. Serve hot garnished with hard-boiled egg.

Shahi Gosht Korma

Creamy lamb cooked in yoghurt

Preparation time: 30 min.
Cooking time: 1 hr.
Serves: 4

Ingredients:

Lamb, rib pieces	500 gm
Ginger (*adrak*) paste	2 tsp / 12 gm
Garlic (*lasan*) paste	2 tsp / 12 gm
Ghee	2 tbsp / 30 gm
White butter	2½ tbsp / 50 gm
Onion, medium, sliced	1
Cinnamon (*dalchini*), 1″ sticks	2
Bay leaves (*tej patta*)	2
Green cardamom (*choti elaichi*) powder	1 tsp
Yoghurt (*dahi*)	¼ cup / 45 gm
Almond (*badam*) paste	1 tbsp / 15 gm
Salt to taste	
Cream	2 tbsp / 40 ml
Wholemilk fudge (*khoa*)	1 tbsp / 15 gm
White pepper (*safed mirch*) powder	½ tsp / 1 gm
Saffron (*kesar*), dissolved in 1 tbsp water (see p. 7)	a few strands

Method:

1. Marinate the lamb with ginger and garlic pastes for at least 30 minutes.
2. Heat the ghee in a pan; add the white butter, onion, cinnamon sticks, bay leaves, and green cardamom powder. Sauté till the onion turns brown. Add the lamb, mix well, and cook on high heat for 5 minutes or till the lamb is browned.
3. Add the yoghurt and almond paste; cook for 40-45 minutes on a low flame or till the lamb is tender.
4. Add the remaining ingredients and mix thoroughly. Serve hot.

Tandoori Murgh

Roast chicken

Preparation time: 3-4 hrs.
Cooking time: 30 min.
Serves: 4

Ingredients:

Chicken, broiler	500 gm
For the marinade:	
Yoghurt (*dahi*)	½ cup / 90 gm
Cumin (*jeera*) powder	1 tsp / 1½ gm
Garam masala (see p. 6)	2 tsp / 4 gm
Ginger (*adrak*) paste	5 tsp / 30 gm
Lemon (*nimbu*) juice	2 tbsp / 30 ml
Vegetable oil	3½ tbsp / 52 ml
Red chilli paste	1 tsp / 5 gm
Saffron (*kesar*)	a few strands
Salt to taste	
Lemon (*nimbu*), cut into wedges	1
Onion, cut into rings	1

Method:

1. Clean the chicken, remove the skin and make 3 incisions each on the breasts, thighs, and legs.
2. Whisk the yoghurt in a large bowl, add all the ingredients for the marinade. Add the chicken and coat well. Keep aside to marinate for 3-4 hours.
3. Preheat the tandoor or oven to 175°C. Skewer the chicken, leaving 4 cm gap between each piece. Keep a tray underneath to collect the drippings.
4. If one is using a *tandoor*, take the chicken out from the *tandoor* when nearly half ready for about 10 minutes and then put it back in the *tandoor* till the chicken is done. If cooking in the oven then there is no need to take the chicken out.
5. Serve hot garnished with lemon and onion.

Murgh Mussalam

Chicken in a yoghurt-based curry

Preparation time: 2 hrs.
Cooking time: 2 hrs.
Serves: 6

Ingredients:

Chicken, cut into 8 pieces	1 kg
Juice of lemon (*nimbu*)	1
Ghee	1 tbsp / 15 gm
Onions, sliced	1 cup / 240 gm
Ginger (*adrak*), 1″ piece, chopped	1
Yoghurt (*dahi*)	1 cup / 180 gm
Almonds (*badam*), ground	12
Raisins (*kishmish*)	10-12
Garam masala (see p. 6)	1 tsp / 2 gm
Saffron (*kesar*)	a few strands
Lemon (*nimbu*), cut into wedges	1
Onion, cut into rings	1
Green coriander (*hara dhaniya*), chopped	

Method:

1. Mix the lemon juice with the chicken and keep aside to marinate for 2 hours.
2. Heat the ghee in a wok (*kadhai*); add the onions and ginger; sauté till brown. Remove and keep aside to cool. Then grind into a smooth paste.
3. In the same wok add the chicken and sauté lightly.
4. Blend the yoghurt, onion-ginger paste, and almond paste together. Add to the chicken, cook covered with a heavy lid containing some water. This is *dum pukht* (see p. 93) cooking.
5. After about 30 minutes, add raisins, *garam* masala, and saffron; cook for 1½ hours more.
6. Serve garnished with lemon, onion, and green coriander.

Dum Murgh

Chicken in a rich creamy sauce

Preparation time: 30 min.
Cooking time: 1 hr.
Serves: 8

Ingredients:

Chicken, small, cut into small pieces	2 (500 gm each)
Juice of lemon (*nimbu*)	1
Ghee	2 tbsp / 30 gm
Butter	2 tbsp / 40 gm
Bay leaves (*tej patta*)	2-3
Cloves (*laung*)	8
Green cardamoms (*choti elaichi*)	8
Cinnamon (*dalchini*), 1″ sticks	3-4
Onions, ground	½ cup / 120 gm
Ginger (*adrak*) paste	1 tsp / 6 gm
Garlic (*lasan*) paste	1 tsp / 6 gm
Almond (*badam*) paste	½ cup / 100 gm
Green chillies, slit	4
Mace (*javitri*), powdered	2-3 blades
Cream, fresh	½ cup / 100 ml
Saffron (*kesar*), soaked in 1 tbsp water (see p. 7)	a few strands
Salt to taste	
Red chilli powder	2 tsp / 4 gm
Mint (*pudina*) leaves	20

Method:

1. Marinate the chicken in lemon juice for 30 minutes.
2. Heat the ghee and butter in a pan; add the bay leaves, cloves, green cardamoms, and cinnamon sticks; sauté over medium heat till they crackle.

3. Add the onion paste, sauté for 3-4 minute; add the ginger paste, garlic paste, and almond paste. Cook over medium heat till the oil separates.
4. Add the chicken and cook for about 10 minutes.
5. Add the green chillies, mace powder, cream, saffron, salt, and red chilli powder. Mix well.
6. Sprinkle some mint leaves, cover the pan with a heavy lid and seal with dough. Keep on a small charcoal fire with live embers on the lid and cook for at least 45 minutes to an hour.

Juicy Meat

While marinating meat, add a little oil to the marinade to keep the meat juicy and succulent.

Khusroe-e-Tursh

Chicken breasts stuffed with cottage cheese

Preparation time: 30 min.
Cooking time: 1 hr.
Serves: 10

Ingredients:

Chicken breasts, boneless	10
For the filling:	
Cottage cheese (*paneer*)	250 gm
Ginger (*adrak*), 1″ piece, ground	1
Garlic (*lasan*), ground	6 cloves
Black cumin (*shah jeera*) seeds, powdered	2 tsp
Onions, sliced	¾ cup / 200 gm
Capsicum (*Shimla mirch*), shredded	75 gm
Mint (*pudina*) leaves	10
Yoghurt (*dahi*), hung for 2 hours	250 gm
Almond (*badam*) paste	4 tbsp / 60 gm
Saffron (*kesar*)	a few strands
Garam masala (see p. 6)	1 tsp / 2 gm
Cream	1¼ cups / 250 ml
Ghee	1¼ cups / 250 gm
Salt to taste	
Green chillies	3

Method:

1. Make a pocket on the side of each chicken breast.
2. **For the filling**, mash the cottage cheese and mix in the remaining filling ingredients.
3. Stuff this filling in the chicken pockets.
4. Mix the almond paste, saffron, *garam* masala, and cream together.
5. Heat the ghee in a pan; add the stuffed chicken breasts, almond mixture, salt, and green chillies. Cook on *dum* (see p. 93) for about 15-20 minutes.
6. Serve hot with a dash of lemon juice.

Machchi Methi

Fish flavoured with fenugreek

Preparation time: 15 min.
Cooking time: 20 min.
Serves: 2-4

Ingredients:

Fish, Rahu or any other variety, washed, dried	500 gm
Vegetable oil	½ tbsp / 7½ ml
Fenugreek seeds (*methi dana*)	½ tsp / 1½ gm
Coriander (*dhaniya*) powder	2 tsp / 3 gm
Cumin (*jeera*) seeds	1 tsp / 2 gm
Turmeric (*haldi*) powder	½ tsp / 1 gm
Red chilli powder	1 tsp / 2 gm
Yoghurt (*dahi*), hung	1 cup / 180 gm
Onion, medium, ground	1
Ginger (*adrak*), 1″ piece, ground	1
Fenugreek (*methi*) leaves	1 small bunch
or	
Dry fenugreek leaves (*kasoori methi*)	1 tsp / ½ gm

Method:

1. Heat the oil in a pan; add the fenugreek seeds. When the seeds turn black remove them from the oil and discard. Now add the remaining ingredients and sauté till the oil separates.
2. Add the washed fish, mix gently and cook on *dum* (see p. 93) for about 15 minutes.
3. Serve hot with steamed rice.

Tandoori Machchi

Tangy grilled fish

Preparation time: 4-5 hrs.
Cooking time: 15 min.
Serves: 6-8

Ingredients:

Fish, Pomfret, fillets cut thick	4 (400 gm each)
For the marinade:	
Vinegar (*sirka*)	1/3 cup / 65 ml
Ginger (*adrak*), chopped	1 tbsp / 24 gm
Garlic (*lasan*), cloves	4
Salt to taste	
Coriander (*dhaniya*) powder	2 tsp / 3 gm
Cumin (*jeera*) seeds	1 tsp / 2 gm
Yellow chillies, ground	½ tsp
Vegetable oil	½ cup / 100 ml
Vegetable oil for basting	
Onions, cut into rings	2
Lemon (*nimbu*), cut into wedges	2
Chaat masala (see p. 6) to taste	

Method:

1. **For the marinade**, grind all the ingredients to a smooth paste. Marinate the fish with this paste for at least 4-5 hours.
2. Wipe and oil the skewer before inserting it through the fish fillets.
3. Now roast the skewered fish in the *tandoor*, with the skewer standing upright (to allow drippings to fall off), for about 5 minutes.
4. Then baste with oil; cook for another 5 minutes or till done.
5. Remove the fish from the skewer; serve garnished with onion rings and lemon wedges, and sprinkled with *chaat* masala.

Khatta Meetha Kaddu

Sweet and sour pumpkin

Preparation time: 10 min.
Cooking time: 30 min.
Serves: 8

Ingredients:

Pumpkin (*kaddu*), peeled, cut into cubes	1 kg
Ghee	1 tbsp / 15 gm
Bay leaf (*tej patta*)	1
Cumin (*jeera*) seeds	1 tsp / 2 gm
Coriander (*dhaniya*) seeds	1 tsp / 2 gm
Fenugreek seeds (*methi dana*)	1 tsp / 3 gm
Fennel (*moti saunf*), powdered	1 tsp / 2 gm
Onion seeds (*kalonji*)	½ tsp / ¾ gm
Asafoetida (*hing*)	a pinch
Ginger (*adrak*) paste	1″ piece
Turmeric (*haldi*) powder	½ tsp / 1 gm
Dry red chillies (*sookhi lal mirch*)	2
Salt to taste	
Coriander (*dhaniya*) powder	2 tsp / 3 gm
Jaggery (*gur*)	a small lump
Tamarind (*imli*) pulp (see p. 7)	2 tbsp / 12 gm
Garam masala (see p. 6)	1 tsp / 2 gm
Green chillies	2-3
Green coriander (*hara dhaniya*)	2 tbsp / 8 gm

Method:

1. Heat the ghee in a pan; add the next seven ingredients and sauté for 1 minute. Add the ginger paste and pumpkin; stir-fry for another 2 minutes.
2. Mix in the turmeric powder, dry red chillies, and salt. Add coriander powder and cook covered, on low heat, for 15 minutes or till half done.
3. Add jaggery, tamarind juice, *garam* masala, and green chillies. Cover and cook, on low heat, till done. Garnish with green coriander and serve.

Aloo Ki Khatti Tarkari

Easy-to-make potato dish

Preparation time: 20 min.
Cooking time: 4 min.
Serves: 2

Ingredients:

Potatoes, boiled, mashed roughly	250 gm
Vegetable oil	1 tbsp / 15 ml
Asafoetida (*hing*)	a pinch
Ginger (*adrak*), 1″ piece, julienned	1
Turmeric (*haldi*) powder	¼ tsp / ½ gm
Coriander (*dhaniya*) powder	1 tsp / 1½ gm
Cumin (*jeera*) powder	1 tsp / 1½ gm
Tomato purée, fresh (see p. 6)	1¼ cups / 250 ml
Salt to taste	
Green chillies	2
Dry red chillies (*sookhi lal mirch*)	3

Method:

1. Heat the oil in the pan; add asafoetida, ginger, turmeric powder, coriander powder, and cumin powder. Sauté for a while.
2. Add the potatoes and sauté for 1 minute. Add the tomato purée, salt, and green chillies. Cook for 2 minutes.
3. Garnish with dry red chillies and serve with *khasta kachauri* (see p. 8) or *bharvin puri* (see p. 54).

Sookhe Kabuli Chane

Spicy chickpeas cooked dry

Preparation time: 10 min.+ overnight
Cooking time: 1 hr.
Serves: 4

Ingredients:

Ingredient	Quantity
Chickpeas (*kabuli chana*)	1½ cups / 250 gm
Bicarbonate of soda	1 tsp / 6 gm
Tea bag	1
Coriander (*dhaniya*) seeds	2 tbsp / 12 gm
Cumin (*jeera*) seeds	1 tbsp / 6 gm
Red chilli powder	1 tsp / 2 gm
Pomegranate seeds (*anar dana*), ground	2 tsp / 4 gm
Mango powder (*amchur*)	2 tbsp / 8 gm
Garam masala (see p. 6)	2 tsp / 4 gm
Salt to taste	
Potatoes, cut into fingers, fried	2
Ginger (*adrak*), 2″ piece, julienned, fried	1
Vegetable oil	½ cup / 100 ml
Green chillies	2
Dry red chillies (*sookhi lal mirch*), chopped	1
Onions, cut into rings	1

Method:

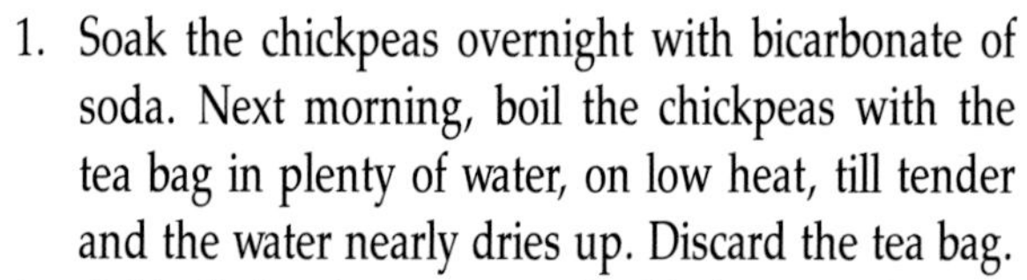

1. Soak the chickpeas overnight with bicarbonate of soda. Next morning, boil the chickpeas with the tea bag in plenty of water, on low heat, till tender and the water nearly dries up. Discard the tea bag.
2. Add all the dry spices, salt, fried potato fingers, and ginger; toss well.
3. Heat the oil in a pan; add the chickpea mixture, and toss on low heat for about 10 minutes.
4. Serve hot garnished with green chillies, dry red chillies, and onions rings.

Dum Karela

Bitter gourd cooked on a slow fire

Preparation time: 15 min.
Cooking time: 45 min.
Serves: 5-6

Ingredients:

Ingredient	Quantity
Bitter gourd (*karela*), scraped, sliced into 4 pieces, deseeded	10 pieces
Mustard (*sarson*) oil	½ cup / 100 ml
Potatoes, sliced	3
Ghee	½ cup / 95 gm
Asafoetida (*hing*)	a pinch
Cumin (*jeera*) seeds	1 tsp / 2 gm
Fenugreek seeds (*methi dana*)	¼ tsp / ¾ gm
Green chillies, finely chopped	4
Jaggery (*gur*)	a small piece
Onion seeds (*kalonji*)	¼ tsp
Yoghurt (*dahi*), beaten	1 cup / 180 gm
Ginger powder (*sonth*)	½ tsp / 1 gm
Coriander (*dhaniya*) powder	1 tsp / 1½ gm
Salt to taste	
Red chilli powder to taste	
Ginger (*adrak*), 1″ piece, crushed	1
Green coriander (*hara dhaniya*), chopped	a bunch

Method:

1. Heat the mustard oil in a wok (*kadhai*); fry the bitter gourd. Remove and keep aside. Fry the potatoes till golden. Remove and keep aside.
2. In another wok, heat the ghee. Add the asafoetida, cumin seeds, fenugreek seeds, green chillies, jaggery, and onion seeds. When they splutter, add the fried potatoes and bitter gourd; mix well.
3. Add the yoghurt, the remaining spices and ginger. Cook on *dum* (see p. 93) for 30 minutes. When soft, add green coriander and serve hot.

Shahi Salan

Mixed vegetables for the Royals

Preparation time: 1 hr.
Cooking time: 45 min.
Serves: 10-12

Ingredients:

Ingredient	Quantity
Bengal gram (*chana dal*), soaked for 1 hour	1 cup / 160 gm
Okra (*bhindi*), chopped, fried	200 gm
Potatoes, diced, fried	100 gm
Carrots (*gajar*), diced, fried	100 gm
French beans, diced, fried	100 gm
Green peas (*matar*), shelled, fried	200 gm
Cottage cheese (*paneer*), diced, fried	100 gm
Ghee	2 tbsp / 30 gm
Ginger (*adrak*), 1″ piece, finely chopped	1
Garlic (*lasan*) pod, minced	1
Cumin (*jeera*) powder	1½ tsp / 2 gm
Coriander (*dhaniya*) powder	1 tsp / 1½ gm
Turmeric (*haldi*) powder	½ tsp / 1 gm
Salt to taste	
Sugar	2 tsp / 6 gm
Tomato purée (see p. 6)	2 cups / 400 ml
Juice of lemon (*nimbu*)	1
Garam masala (see p. 6)	1 tsp / 2 gm
Mango powder (*amchur*)	1 tsp / 2 gm

Method:

1. Drain and boil the Bengal gram in 1½ cups water.
2. Heat the ghee in a pan; add ginger, garlic, all the fried vegetables, cottage cheese, boiled Bengal gram, cumin, coriander, and turmeric powders. Sauté for 2-3 minutes. Mix the salt and sugar with the tomato purée, and pour over the vegetables.
3. Add the remaining ingredients; cook on *dum* (see p. 93) for 30 minutes. Serve hot.

Sarson Ka Saag

Spicy mustard greens

Preparation time: 30 min.
Cooking time: 45 min.
Serves: 6-8

Ingredient:

Mustard (*sarson*) leaves, cleaned, washed, chopped	1 kg
Spinach (*palak*), chopped	500 gm
Turnip (*shalgam*), chopped	1
Dill (*soy saag*), chopped	200 gm
Radish (*mooli*) leaves, chopped	4-5
Maize flour (*makkai ka atta*)	1 tbsp / 10 gm
Salt to taste	
Ghee	3 tbsp / 45 gm
Asafoetida (*hing*)	a pinch
Ginger (*adrak*), julienned	100 gm
Garlic (*lasan*), cloves	100 gm
Green chillies, slit	3-4

Method:

1. Boil 1 cup water in a pan, add the mustard leaves, spinach, turnip, dill, and radish leaves. Cook for 30 minutes till the water evaporates. Remove and keep aside to cool.
2. Dry roast the maize flour for a few minutes till a good fragrance emanates.
3. Blend the leaves in a blender. Transfer the contents in a pan, add the maize flour and salt; cook till it begins to leave the sides of the pan.
4. Heat the ghee in another pan; add the asafoetida, ginger, garlic, and green chillies. Sauté for a while. Add this to the green mixture; mix well.
5. Serve with 1 tsp of fresh white butter accompanied with *makkai ki roti* (see p. 63).

Janat-e-Numa

Stuffed potatoes in spinach sauce

Preparation time: 20 min.
Cooking time: 35 min.
Serves: 10

Ingredients:

Potatoes	1 kg
Mustard oil for frying	
For the filling:	
Mint (*pudina*) leaves	100 gm
Green coriander (*hara dhaniya*)	250 gm
Green chillies	50 gm
Cumin (*jeera*) seeds	1 tsp / 2 gm
Mango powder (*amchur*)	5 tsp / 10 gm
Raisins (*kishmish*)	cup / 50 gm
Salt to taste	
Mustard oil	cup / 100 ml
Turmeric (*haldi*) powder	2 tsp / 5 gm
Tomatoes, finely chopped	200 gm
Spinach (*palak*), washed	1 kg
Fenugreek (*methi*) leaves, washed	250 gm
Red chilli powder	10 tsp / 20 gm
Salt to taste	
Coriander (*dhaniya*) powder	5 tsp / 7 gm
Garam masala (see p. 6)	5 tsp / 10 gm
Yoghurt (*dahi*)	cup / 90 gm
Ghee	2 tbsp / 30 gm
Green coriander (*hara dhaniya*), chopped	2 tbsp / 8 gm
Ginger (*adrak*), íí piece, julienned	1

Method:

1. Peel and scoop out the inside portion of the potatoes, leaving the outer skin intact.
2. Heat the mustard oil till smoking in a wok (*kadhai*); deep-fry the potato shells till crisp and golden.

Remove with a slotted spoon and drain the excess oil on absorbent kitchen paper towels.

3. **For the filling**, blend all the ingredients together to a smooth paste. Keep aside.
4. Heat the oil till smoking in the same wok; add the turmeric powder, tomatoes, spinach, and fenugreek leaves. Sauté for 15 minutes or till the mixture thickens.
5. Remove from heat and keep aside to cool. When cool, blend this spinach mixture.
6. Fill the fried potato shells with the mint and coriander paste and put them on a frying pan.
7. Pour the spinach gravy over the stuffed potatoes. Add red chilli powder, salt, coriander powder, *garam* masala, yoghurt, and ghee and cook the potatoes on *dum* (see p. 93) for about 1 hour.
8. Serve hot garnished with green coriander and ginger.

Note: *Mustard oil should be heated to smoking point and then cooled before adding the other ingredients.*

Kesar-e-Paneer

Cottage cheese in a thick tomato gravy

Preparation time: 15 min.
Cooking time: 20 min.
Serves: 4-6

Ingredients:

Cottage cheese (*paneer*), cut into ½" cubes	700 gm
Tomatoes, chopped	1 kg
Ginger (*adrak*), chopped	1 tbsp / 24 gm
Garlic (*lasan*), chopped	2 tbsp / 24 gm
Red chilli powder	5 tsp / 10 gm
Green cardamoms (*choti elaichi*)	2 gm
Ghee	¾ cup / 150 gm
Mace (*javitri*), powdered	1 tsp / 2 gm
Salt and black pepper powder to taste	
Garam masala (see p. 6)	5 tsp / 10 gm
Butter	5 tbsp / 100 gm
Cream	½ cup / 100 ml
Saffron (*kesar*), soaked, blended in 2 tsp water	a few strands

Method:

1. Boil the tomatoes with ginger, garlic, red chilli powder, and green cardamoms. When the tomatoes turn soft, remove and keep aside to cool. Squeeze out the pulp; strain the tomato mixture.
2. Heat the ghee in a pan; add the tomato purée and the cottage cheese; let the mixture simmer for 10 minutes. Add mace powder, salt, black pepper powder, and *garam* masala; cook for 4-5 minutes.
3. Add the butter, and when it begins to melt add the cream. Mix well.
4. Add the saffron water and blend thoroughly.
5. Serve hot with a swirl of cream.

Sookhi Dal

Black gram cooked dry

Preparation time: 20 min.+ overnight
Cooking time: 10 min.
Serves: 3-4

Ingredients:

Split black gram (*dhuli urad dal*), soaked overnight	1 cup / 150 gm
Ghee	1 tbsp / 15 gm
Cumin (*jeera*) seeds	1 tsp / 2 gm
Green chillies, slit	4
Onion, sliced, fried	1
Garam masala (see p. 6)	¼ tsp / ½ gm
Mango powder (*amchur*)	1 tsp / 2 gm
Black pepper (*kali mirch*) powder	½ tsp / 1 gm
Salt to taste	

Method:

1. Rub the split black gram with your hands to remove the skin. Drain.
2. Heat the ghee in a pan; add the cumin seeds and green chillies. When they start spluttering, add the black gram and salt; stir-fry for 4-5 minutes.
3. Pour 2 cups water; cook on a high flame till little water remains. Lower the flame and simmer till the grains are cooked and the mixture is dry. Stir gently and occasionally so that the grains don't break and stick to the bottom of the pan.
4. Transfer to a bowl; garnish with fried onion, *garam* masala, mango powder, and black pepper powder. A dollop of butter or 1 tbsp of hot ghee can be added to enhance the flavour.

Khatti Tur Dal

Tangy red gram

Preparation time: 10 min.
Cooking time: 40 min.
Serves: 2-4

Ingredients:

Split red gram (*arhar dal*)	1 cup / 160 gm
Water	3 cups / 600 ml
Turmeric (*haldi*) powder	½ tsp / 1 gm
Salt to taste	
Grind to a paste	
Ginger (*adrak*), 1″ piece	1
Garlic (*lasan*), cloves	5
Black peppercorns (*sabut kali mirch*)	8
Cinnamon (*dalchini*), 1″ stick	1
Coriander (*dhaniya*) seeds	1 tsp / 2 gm
Cumin (*jeera*) seeds	1 tsp / 2 gm
Green chillies, slit	4
Ghee	2 tbsp / 30 gm
Asafoetida (*hing*)	1 grain
Sugar / Jaggery (*gur*)	1 tsp / 3 gm
Tomatoes, blanched, seeds removed	2
Juice of lemon (*nimbu*)	1
Green coriander (*hara dhaniya*), chopped	1 bunch

Method:

1. Boil the split red gram in water with turmeric powder and salt for 25 minutes or till a thick soup-like consistency is obtained.
2. Grind the ingredients mentioned to a fine paste.
3. Heat the ghee in a pan; add the asafoetida, sugar / jaggery, and tomatoes; sauté for 2 minutes. Add the paste and stir-fry for 5 minutes on low heat.
4. Add the red gram and cook till thick. Mix in the lemon juice. Serve garnished with green coriander.

Dal Makhani

Rich and creamy black gram

Preparation time: 10 min.
Cooking time: 2 hrs.
Serves: 4

Ingredients:

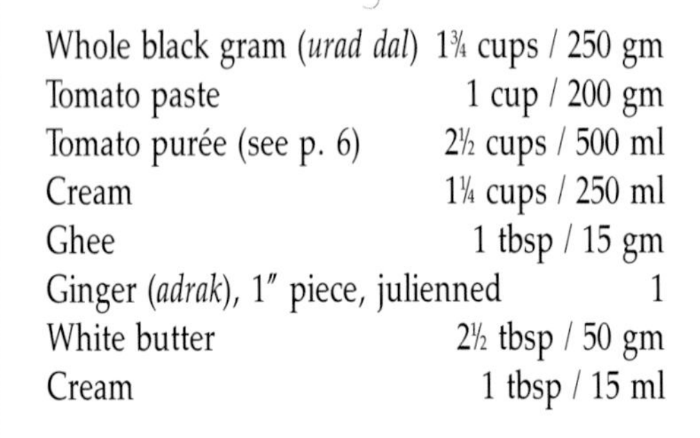

Whole black gram (*urad dal*)	1¾ cups / 250 gm
Tomato paste	1 cup / 200 gm
Tomato purée (see p. 6)	2½ cups / 500 ml
Cream	1¼ cups / 250 ml
Ghee	1 tbsp / 15 gm
Ginger (*adrak*), 1″ piece, julienned	1
White butter	2½ tbsp / 50 gm
Cream	1 tbsp / 15 ml

Method:

1. In a heavy-bottomed pan, boil 6 cups water. Add the black gram and cook on a medium flame till the grains are just a little tender and begin to split.
2. Add the tomato paste, tomato purée, and cream; simmer (adding hot water if necessary) for 2 hours or more till the black gram is soft and the mixture turns a rich red in colour.
3. Heat the ghee in a wok (*kadhai*); sauté the ginger and add to the black gram mixture.
4. Add a dollop of white butter; serve hot garnished with a swirl of cream.

Bharvin Puri

Black gram-stuffed fried bread

Preparation time: 10 min.+ overnight
Cooking time: 20 min.
Serves: 6-8

Ingredients:

Wholewheat flour (*atta*)	5 cups / 500 gm
Salt to taste	
Vegetable oil	2 tbsp / 30 ml
For the stuffing:	
Whole black gram (*urad dal*), soaked overnight, drained	1 cup / 150 gm
Asafoetida (*hing*)	a pinch
Fennel (*moti saunf*), pounded	1 tbsp / 6 gm
Coriander (*dhaniya*) seeds, crushed	4 tsp / 8 gm
Red chilli powder	1 tsp / 2 gm
Vegetable oil for frying	

Method:

1. Sift the flour and salt. Mix in the oil and knead with enough water to make a smooth dough.
2. **For the stuffing,** remove the skin of the black gram by rubbing between your palms. Grind the black gram with all the spices to a coarse, sticky paste.
3. Divide the flour dough equally into 20 balls. Flatten each ball, grease the top surface and add 1 tbsp paste. Bring the edges together to seal the filling. Make a ball and roll each out to a 3″disc. Repeat with the other balls.
4. Heat the oil in a wok (*kadhai*); deep-fry the discs, on low heat, till golden on both sides. Remove and drain. Before serving, fry the puffs again till crisp.
5. Serve hot with *aloo ki khatti tarkari* (see p. 38)

Aloo Paratha

Potato-stuffed leavened bread

Preparation time: 10 min.
Cooking time: 30 min.
Serves: 4-5

Ingredients:

Wholewheat flour (*atta*)	½ cup / 50 gm
Ghee	1 tbsp / 15 gm
For the filling:	
Potatoes, boiled, mashed	1 cup
Garam masala (see p. 6)	½ tsp / 1 gm
Red chilli powder	¾ tsp/ 1½ gm
Coriander (*dhaniya*) seeds, roasted, powdered	1 tsp / 2 gm
Green coriander (*hara dhaniya*), chopped	1 tbsp / 4 gm
Onion, chopped	1 tbsp / 12 gm
Salt to taste	
Ghee for shallow frying	

Method:

1. Sift the wholewheat flour. Rub in the ghee with the fingertips. Knead with enough cold water to make a soft dough.
2. **For the filling**, mix all the ingredients together. Divide the filling into 10 equal portions.
3. Divide the dough equally into 10 portions. Flatten each out into a small disc. Place 1 portion of the filling in the centre, press the edges to seal and reshape into a ball. Roll each ball out into an 8″ disc, dusting with dry flour to prevent sticking.
4. Heat a griddle (*tawa*); cook the disc, drizzling 1 tsp ghee, till tiny brown spots appear on both sides. Similarly repeat with the other discs.
5. Serve hot with yoghurt, chutney and pickle.

Methi Ki Roti

Fenugreek-flavoured leavened bread

Preparation time: 40 min.
Cooking time: 15 min.
Serves: 2-3

Ingredients:

Wholewheat flour (*atta*)	2 cups / 200 gm
Fenugreek (*methi*) leaves, chopped	1¾ cups / 50 gm
Green coriander (*hara dhaniya*), chopped	1 cup / 25 gm
Green chillies, chopped	2
Salt to taste	
Vegetable oil for frying	

Method:

1. Mix the wholewheat flour, fenugreek leaves, green coriander, green chillies, and salt together. Add 1 tbsp oil; knead with enough water to make a smooth dough. Cover and keep aside for 30 minutes.
2. Knead again and divide the dough into lemon-sized balls. Roll each out to a 2″ disc, smear some oil on the top surface and fold into a half moon. Fold the half moon again into a triangle. Now roll the triangle out.
3. Heat a griddle (*tawa*); lay a triangle flat on it and cook on both sides till tiny brown spots appear. Drizzle a little oil and fry till golden brown on both sides. Remove and repeat till all the triangles are fried.
4. Serve hot with yoghurt and pickle of your choice.

Tandoori Roti

Baked leavened bread

Preparation time: 40 min.
Cooking time: 6 min.
Serves: 2-3

Ingredients:

Wholewheat flour (*atta*)	2½ cups / 250 gm
Salt	1 tsp / 4 gm
Vegetable oil	1 tbsp / 15 ml
Water	½ cup / 100 ml
Butter to grease baking tray	

Method:

1. Sift the flour and salt together. Mix in the oil and water; knead to make a soft dough. Cover with a moist cloth and keep aside for 30 minutes.
2. Divide the dough equally into 5 balls and dust with flour.
3. Heat the oven to 175°C; flatten the balls and roll each out to an 8″ disc. Place the discs on a greased tray and bake for 3 minutes till pale brown in colour.
4. Serve hot.

(Photograph on facing page, front)

Badshahi Naan

Deep-fried flour bread

Preparation time: 30 min.
Cooking time: 20 min.
Serves: 6

Ingredients:

Refined flour (*maida*)	10 cups / 1 kg
Yeast, granulated	2 tsp / 8 gm
Sugar	2 tsp / 6 gm
Water, lukewarm	1 cup / 200 ml
Butter	4 tsp / 20 gm
Milk, warm	1 cup / 180 ml
Eggs, beaten	2
Onion seeds (*kalonji*)	1 tsp / 1½ gm
Salt to taste	
Ghee for deep-frying	

(Photograph on page 61, back)

Method:

1. Mix the yeast, sugar, and water together. Keep aside for 10 minutes.
2. Sift the flour and salt. Rub in the butter till the mixture becomes crumbly.
3. Add the yeast mixture, milk, and eggs; knead into a smooth, elastic dough. Cover with a damp cloth and keep in a warm place to rise. It should rise to almost double its volume.
4. Knead again and divide the dough into 16 balls. Roll each out into a ¾"-thick disc. Lay the discs on a greased tray; sprinkle the onion seeds. Let the discs rise again till they double in size.
5. Deep-fry the discs in a wok till golden brown. Remove and drain the excess oil. Serve hot.

Makkai Ki Roti

Maize flour bread

Preparation time: 10 min.
Cooking time: 40 min.
Serves: 4-6

Ingredients:

Maize flour (*makkai ka atta*)	2½ cups / 500 gm
Salt to taste	
Ghee	1 tbsp / 15 gm
Fenugreek (*methi*) leaves, finely chopped	1 cup / 30 gm
Red chilli powder	1 tsp / 2 gm
Ghee for frying	2 tbsp / 30 gm
Butter	1 tbsp / 20 gm

Method:

1. Sift the maize flour and salt. Add the ghee, fenugreek leaves, and red chilli powder; mix well. Make a stiff dough with hot water.
2. Divide the dough into 8-10 portions. Shape each out into a thick disc between your palms.
3. Heat the griddle (*tawa*) till hot; lay the disc flat on it and cook both sides on low heat.
4. When nearly done, pour a little ghee and fry both sides till golden brown. Remove from the griddle and pinch the disc in four or five places on one side. Add butter on the pinched places and serve hot. Repeat with the other discs.
5. Serve with *sarson ka saag* (see p. 44).

Kesari Pulao

Sweet saffron rice with almonds and raisins

Preparation time: 20 min.
Cooking time: 10 min.
Serves: 2-3

Ingredients:

Rice	1 cup / 200 gm
Ghee	2 tbsp / 30 gm
Sugar	3 tbsp / 60 gm
Almonds (*badam*), blanched	10
Raisins (*kishmish*), washed, lightly fried	30
Dry coconut (*copra*), cut in ½ cm cubes, lightly fried	1 tbsp / 4 gm
Green cardamoms (*choti elaichi*), skinned, seeds crushed coarsely	6
Saffron (*kesar*), soaked in 3 tbsp hot milk	a few strands

Method:

1. Cook the rice in a pan till half done. Drain and keep aside to cool.
2. Heat 1 tbsp ghee in another pan; add the rice and mix well. Add the sugar, almonds, raisins, coconut, and green cardamom powder; mix well.
3. Pour the saffron mixture over the rice.
4. Heat the remaining ghee and mix with the rice. Cover the pan with a heavy lid; keep some hot ashes on it and a few live embers under the pan for 10-15 minutes till the rice is completely done and the grains are separated. Alternately, bake in a moderate oven for 10 minutes.

Note: *The rice is eaten as a dessert on festive occasions.*

Biryani-e-Dum Pukht

Flavoured rice cooked with lamb

Preparation time: 1 hr.
Cooking time: 2 hrs.
Serves: 6-8

Ingredients:

Lamb	1 kg
For the rice:	
Rice, Basmati	2½ cups / 500 gm
Green cardamoms (*choti elaichi*)	6
Cloves (*laung*)	10
Cinnamon (*dalchini*), 1″ sticks	2
Cumin (*jeera*) seeds	1 tsp / 2 gm
Nutmeg (*jaiphal*)	½
Mace (*javitri*)	3-4 blades
Water	10 cups / 2 lt
Bay leaves (*tej patta*)	5
Saffron (*kesar*), mixed with 1 tbsp water or milk	a few strands
Garlic (*lasan*)	50 gm
Ginger (*adrak*), 1″ piece	1
Ghee	1¼ cups / 250 gm
Onions, sliced	2 tbsp / 25 gm
Cloves, powdered	1 tsp / 2 gm
Mace	3 gm
Cinnamon sticks, powdered	1 tsp / 2 gm
Green cardamoms, powdered	5
Salt to taste	
Yoghurt (*dahi*)	¾ cup / 135 gm
Yellow chilli powder	2 tsp / 5 gm
Saffron (*kesar*)	a few strands
Mint (*pudina*) leaves	1 sprig
Vetiver (*kewda*) essence	1 tsp / 5 ml
Onions, medium, sliced, browned	2
Black cumin (*shah jeera*) seeds	1 tsp / 2 gm
Lemon (*nimbu*) juice	1
Cream	1¼ cups / 250 ml

Method:

1. **For the rice,** tie all the spices except bay leaves, in a muslin cloth. Immerse in water and bring to the boil. Add the rice and bay leaves. Cook till the rice is half done; drain out the water and spread the rice on a tray.
2. Colour half the rice with the saffron mixture. Mix the white and the saffron-coloured rice together. Keep aside.
3. Grind the ginger and garlic and squeeze the extract.
4. Heat the ghee in a pan; brown the onions and keep aside to cool. Then grind and mix with the lamb. Add the ginger-garlic extract.
5. Mix in the powdered cloves, mace, cinnamon, green cardamom, and salt.
6. Cook the lamb in a wok (*kadhai*) till brown. Add the yoghurt and yellow chilli powder. Mix well.
7. Once the gravy thickens, add a little water. When the lamb is tender, remove the lamb pieces, and strain the gravy. Grind the saffron and blend into the cooked lamb.
8. Mix the strained gravy with the lamb.
9. Line the bottom of the pan with ghee, add one layer of rice, then a layer of lamb curry. Repeat till all the rice and curry are used up. The last layer should be of rice.
10. Sprinkle the mint leaves, vetiver essence, fried onions, and black cumin seeds on top of the rice. Add the lemon juice and cream, close the lid tightly and seal with dough.
11. Keep the pan on a slow charcoal fire with a few live charcoals on the lid for about 45 minutes. This is the traditional way of making *biryani*. You can also keep it in the oven for 30 minutes. Serve hot.

Cholia Pulao

Horse gram rice

Preparation time: 20 min.
Cooking time: 30 min.
Serves: 2-4

Ingredients:

Rice, Basmati	1 cup / 200 gm
Horse gram (*cholia*)	1 cup
Vegetable oil	1 tbsp / 15 ml
Ginger (*adrak*), 1″ piece, julienned	1
Cloves (*laung*)	4
Cinnamon (*dalchini*), 1″ stick	1
Black cardamoms (*badi elaichi*)	2
Bay leaves (*tej patta*)	2
Water, hot	2 cups / 400 ml

Method:

1. Heat the oil in a pan; add the ginger, cloves, cinnamon stick, black cardamoms, and bay leaves; sauté for 2 minutes.
2. Add the horse gram, sauté for 3 minutes and then add the rice. Stir-fry for 3-4 minutes.
3. Add the water and bring the mixture to the boil. Cover the pan with a heavy lid and cook on low heat for 20 minutes or till the rice is done.
4. Serve hot with any curry or *raita*.

Yakhni Pulao

Rice with lamb stew

Preparation time: 30 min.
Cooking time: 20 min.
Serves: 6

Ingredients:

Rice, Basmati, soaked for 30 minutes	1 cup / 200 gm
Lamb, cut into big pieces	500 gm
Nutmeg (*jaiphal*)	½
Mace (*javitri*)	4 blades
Ginger (*adrak*), 1″ piece, chopped	1
Cinnamon (*dalchini*), 1″ stick	1
Cloves (*laung*)	6
Coriander (*dhaniya*) seeds	1 tbsp / 6 gm
Ghee	4 tbsp / 60 gm
Onions, finely sliced	2
Cumin (*jeera*) seeds	1 tsp / 2 gm
Cinnamon, 1″ stick	1
Cloves	3
Green cardamoms (*choti elaichi*)	4
Garlic (*lasan*) paste	½ tsp / 3 gm
Ginger paste	½ tsp / 3 gm
Salt to taste	
Yoghurt (*dahi*)	1 cup / 180 gm
Onion, sliced, fried	1 tbsp / 12 gm
Mint (*pudina*) leaves	10

Method:

1. In a muslin cloth tie the nutmeg, mace, ginger, cinnamon stick, cloves, and coriander seeds together. This is called bouquet garni.
2. Heat 4 cups water in a wok (*kadhai*); add the lamb, salt, and the bouquet garni; cook on low heat till the lamb is tender. Then squeeze the bouquet garni and discard it.

3. Remove the lamb pieces, strain the liquid and keep both aside.
4. Heat the ghee in a thick-bottomed pan; add the onion and sauté till brown. Add all the spices, garlic and ginger pastes. Sauté for a few seconds.
5. Add the lamb, salt, and yoghurt; cook till the lamb turns brown.
6. Add the drained rice and mix till the rice is well coated. Pour in the strained liquid, mix well, and cover with a heavy lid. Cook for 15 minutes on *dum* (see p. 93) or bake for 20 minutes in a moderate oven.
7. Garnish with fried onion and mint leaves, and serve hot accompanied with cucumber or mint *raita*. This is a complete meal by itself.

For Tender Flesh

Raw papaya is the best tenderiser for meats.

Nimbu Ka Achar

Preparation time: 2 weeks

Lemon pickle

Ingredients:

Lemons (*nimbu*), washed, wiped, slit in quarters without separating the pieces	2 kg
Juice of lemons (*nimbu*)	1 kg
Sugar	1 cup / 150 gm
Black salt (*kala namak*)	250 gm
Black cardamoms (*badi elaichi*)	25 gm
Black peppercorns (*sabut kali mirch*)	15 gm
Dry red chillies (*sookhi lal mirch*)	25 gm
Cumin (*jeera*) seeds	2 tbsp / 12 gm
Black cumin (*shah jeera*) seeds	2 tbsp / 12 gm
Carom (*ajwain*) seeds	15 gm
Asafoetida (*hing*)	a pinch
Ginger powder (*sonth*)	100 gm

Method:

1. Grind the sugar, black salt, black cardamoms, black pepper, dry red chillies, cumin seeds, black cumin seeds, carom seeds, asafoetida, and ginger powder together to a fine powder.
2. Mix ½ cup lemon juice with the powder and stuff the slit lemons with this powder mixture.
3. Arrange the stuffed lemons in a glass jar, with a layer of the powder mixture between them. Repeat till all the lemons and powder mixture are used up. Pour the remaining lemon juice.
4. Cover with a thick cloth for the first 2 days and then put the jar out in the sun for 2 weeks, shaking occasionally. This pickle aids digestion and can stay for up to 25 years.

Kasundi

Sliced mango pickle

Preparation time: 4 days
Cooking time: 15 min.

Ingredients:

Mangoes, peeled, finely sliced, sun-dried for 4 days	2 kg
Tamarind (*imli*), lemon-sized balls, soaked in 1 cup vinegar for 1 hour	2
Jaggery (*gur*), soaked in 1 cup vinegar	2 cups / 400 gm
Grind to a paste with 4 tbsp vinegar:	
Dry red chillies (*sookhi lal mirch*)	10
Turmeric (*haldi*) powder	2 tbsp
Mustard seeds (*rai*)	100 gm
Ginger (*adrak*), sliced	2 tbsp / 24 gm
Garlic (*lasan*), sliced	1 tbsp / 12 gm
Cumin (*jeera*) seeds	100 gm
Fenugreek seeds (*methi dana*)	100 gm
Gingelly or groundnut oil	2 cups / 400 ml
Garlic (*lasan*), chopped	1 tbsp / 12 gm
Ginger (*adrak*), chopped	2 tbsp / 48 gm
Vinegar (*sirka*)	1¾ cups / 350 ml

Method:

1. Mash the tamarind, strain and keep the extract aside.
2. Cook the jaggery-vinegar mixture till blended.
3. Heat the oil in a wok (*kadhai*); fry the garlic and ginger for 3-4 minutes. Add the ground chilli paste and fry further for 3-4 minutes.
4. Add the mango, jaggery mixture, tamarind extract, and vinegar; cook for 15 minutes till well blended.
5. Add salt if required. Cool and preserve in sterilised jars.

Pudina Chutney

Mint chutney

Preparation time: 5 min.

Ingredients:

Mint (*pudina*) leaves	1 bunch
Green coriander (*hara dhaniya*)	½ bunch
Green chillies	4
Garlic (*lasan*)	1 pod
Salt to taste	
Sugar	1 tsp / 3 gm
Tamarind (*imli*) paste	1 tsp / 3 gm
or	
Juice of lemon (*nimbu*)	1

Method:

1. Grind the mint leaves, green coriander, green chillies, garlic, salt, and sugar to a smooth paste either on a stone slab or in a mixer.
2. Add the tamarind paste or lemon juice, mix well and serve as an accompaniment.

Note: *At different times of the year the pungency of chillies is different, so use your discretion and taste the chillies before putting them in the food.*

Khajoor-Kishmish Chutney

Preparation time: 1 hr. 10 min.

Date and raisin chutney

Ingredients:

Dates (*khajoor*), destoned, cut into strips	500 gm
Raisins (*kishmish*), washed, soaked in hot water	1 cup / 100 gm
Tamarind (*imli*), lemon-sized balls	3
Jaggery (*gur*)	1¼ cups / 250 gm
Water	2 cups / 400 ml
Salt to taste	
Red chilli powder	1 tsp / 2 gm
Cumin (*jeera*) seeds, roasted, powdered	½ tbsp / 3 gm
Ginger powder (*sonth*)	1 tsp / 2 gm

Method:

1. Soak the tamarind and jaggery in water for 30 minutes. Mash the soaked tamarind well and strain removing all the liquid and pulp.
2. Add salt, red chilli powder, cumin powder, and ginger powder. Mix well.
3. Add the dates and drained raisins; mix well.
4. Let it rest for 30 minutes before serving.

Sookhe Aam Ki Chutney

Dried mango chutney

Preparation time: 1 hr.
Cooking time: 10 min.

Ingredients:

Dried mangoes, sliced, soaked for 1 hour	250 gm
Water	2 cups / 400 ml
Jaggery (*gur*)	½ cup / 100 gm
Cumin (*jeera*) seeds	1 tbsp / 6 gm
Asafoetida (*hing*)	a pinch
Black peppercorns (*sabut kali mirch*), powdered	6-7
Black cardamoms (*badi elaichi*), powdered	5-6

Method:

1. Boil the mangoes with water and jaggery; strain.
2. Dry roast the cumin seeds and asafoetida on a griddle (*tawa*) and grind to a fine powder.
3. Add this to the strained mango pulp.
4. Mix in the black pepper powder and black cardamom powder.

Variations: *Raisins and slices of bananas can also be added on festive occasions to this chutney.*

Sonth

Tamarind chutney

Preparation time: 20 min.
Cooking time: 10 min.

Ingredients:

Tamarind (*imli*)	200 gm
Sugar	1 cup / 150 gm
or	
Jaggery (*gur*)	7 tbsp / 150 gm
Ginger (*adrak*), 2" piece, juice extracted	1
Red chilli powder	1 tsp / 2 gm
Black salt (*kala namak*)	¼ tsp / 1 gm
Ginger powder (*sonth*)	1 tsp / 2 gm
Raisins (*kishmish*)	1 tbsp / 10 gm
Juice of lemon (*nimbu*)	½
Green chillies, finely chopped	2
Asafoetida (*hing*)	¼ tsp / 1 gm
Cumin (*jeera*) seeds, dry roasted, ground	1 tbsp / 6 gm

Method:

1. Boil the tamarind, strain the juice and discard the pulp.
2. Add the remaining ingredients and mix well.
3. Serve with *khasta kachauri* (see p. 8) or *chaat papri* (see p. 14).

Variation: *A combination of dates and tamarind or just mango slices can be used instead of just tamarind.*

Note: *Tamarind should always be boiled before straining as it carries a lot of infection.*

Badam Burfee

Almond fudge

Preparation time: 10 min.
Cooking time: 30 min.
Serves: 10-12

Ingredients:

Almonds (*badam*)	4 cups / 500 gm
Sugar	2¾ cups / 400 gm
Water	½ cup / 100 ml
Silver leaves (*varq*)	2-3

Method:

1. Soak the almonds in boiling water for 6-7 minutes. Drain, remove the skin and grind to a coarse paste.
2. Heat the sugar and water together in a pan; stir gently till the sugar dissolves completely. Bring the sugar syrup to the boil and then simmer till bubbles start forming.
3. Add the almond paste and cook, stirring constantly, till the mixture leaves the sides of the pan. Remove from heat.
4. Spread the mixture evenly on a greased plate and smoothen the top. Keep aside to cool and decorate with silver leaves.
5. Cut into squares or diamond shapes and serve.

Shahi Halwa

Semolina pudding

Preparation time: 10 min.
Cooking time: 15 min.
Serves: 2-3

Ingredients:

Semolina (*suji*)	1 cup / 100 gm
Ghee	½ cup / 85 gm
Water	4 cups / 800 ml
Sugar	½ cup / 75 gm
Green cardamoms (*choti elaichi*), crushed	4
Saffron (*kesar*)	a few strands
Almonds (*badam*), blanched, chopped	10

Method:

1. Heat the ghee in a wok (*kadhai*); add the semolina and fry till it is golden brown and a nice aroma emanates.
2. Make a syrup by boiling the water, sugar, green cardamoms, and saffron together for 5 minutes.
3. Mix this syrup with the semolina, stir briskly and cook till the ghee surfaces and the semolina leaves the sides of the pan.
4. Serve hot garnished with almonds.

Variation: *Raisins and cashew nuts can also be added.*

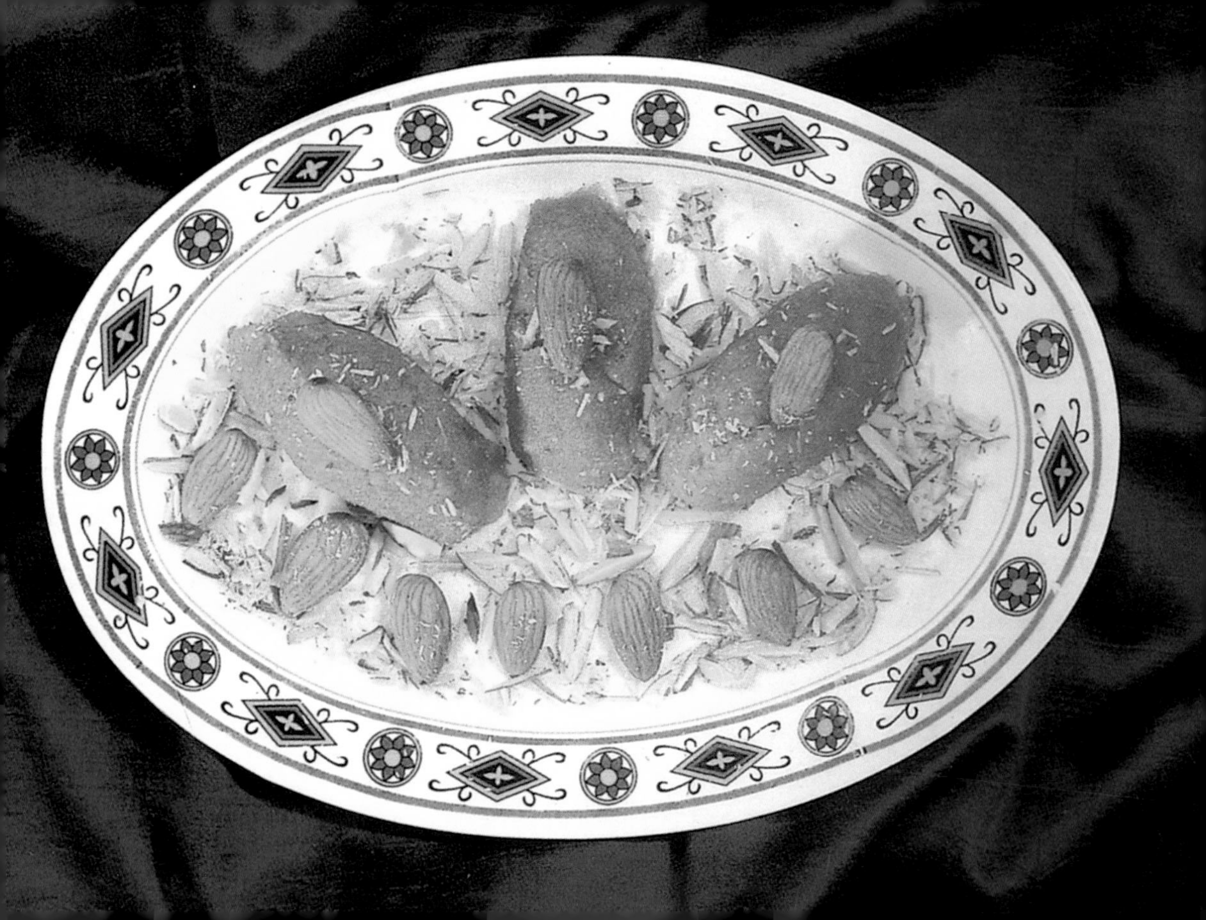

Gajar Halwa

Saffron-flavoured carrot pudding

Preparation time: 30 min.
Cooking time: 1 hr.
Serves: 4

Ingredients:

Carrots (*gajar*), scraped, grated	500 gm
Milk, full cream	8 cups / 1½ lt
Sugar (or to taste)	8 tbsp / 160 gm
Ghee	¾ cup / 150 gm
Green cardamoms (*choti elaichi*), crushed (seeds only)	6
Cashew nuts (*kaju*), chopped	10
Almonds (*badam*), blanched, chopped	10
Saffron (*kesar*), soaked in 1 tsp hot water or milk (see p. 7)	a few strands
Silver leaf (*varq*)	1

Method:

1. Boil the milk and the carrots together on a low flame, till all the milk is absorbed.
2. Add the sugar and ghee; sauté till the carrot turns golden red and the ghee separates.
3. Add the crushed green cardamom seeds, cashew nuts, almonds (keep aside a few dry fruits for the garnish), and saffron; mix well.
4. Serve hot garnished with the remaining dry fruits and silver leaf.

Kulfi

Old-fashioned Indian ice cream

Preparation time: 30 min.
Cooking time: 1 hr. + overnight
Serves: 8

Ingredients:

Milk, full cream	5½ cups / 1 lt
Cream	1¼ cups / 250 ml
Sugar	1⅔ cups / 250 gm
Bread, white	1
Almonds (*badam*), blanched, peeled, roughly ground	20
Pistachios (*pista*)	½ cup
Green cardamoms (*choti elaichi*), crushed	4
Saffron (*kesar*), soaked for 10 minutes (see p. 7)	a few strands

Method:

1. Pour the milk in a thick-bottomed pan; simmer till the milk is reduced to half its original quantity.
2. Cool and add cream, sugar, bread, almonds, pistachios, green cardamoms, and saffron; mix well.
3. Pour into conical *kulfi* moulds and seal tightly with silver foil. Freeze overnight or for at least 12 hours.
4. Just prior to serving, remove the moulds from the freezer. Dip the bottom of the moulds in hot water just for a second, to loosen the sides, and then invert on to serving plates. Serve with *faluda* (cornflour vermicelli).

Phirni

Powdered rice pudding

Preparation time: 1 hr.
Cooking time: 15 min.
Serves: 2-3

Ingredients:

Rice, Basmati, soaked for 1 hour	3 tbsp
Milk, full cream	5½ cups / 1 lt
Sugar	1⅓ cups / 200 gm
Rose water (*gulab jal*)	1 tbsp / 15 ml
Almonds (*badam*), blanched, finely chopped	15
Pistachios (*pista*), finely chopped	10
Saffron (*kesar*), soaked in 1 tbsp water (see p. 7)	10 strands
Green cardamoms (*choti elaichi*), crushed	4-5
Silver leaves (*varq*)	4-5

Method:

1. Grind the rice with ½ cup water.
2. Heat the milk in a pan; add the rice paste and keep stirring till it thickens enough to coat the back of a spoon. Add the sugar and cook till the mixture thickens again to coat the back of the spoon.
3. Remove from heat, transfer the thickened milk into individual earthen containers or glass bowls.
4. Sprinkle rose water and half the dry fruits.
5. Grind the saffron in a mortar and pestle. Sprinkle this over the dry fruits.
6. Garnish with the remaining dry fruits, green cardamom powder and silver leaves. Refrigerate to set. Serve cold.

Rabri Malai-Balai

A rich creamy dessert

Preparation time: 5 min.
Cooking time: 1 hr.
Serves: 12-15

Ingredients:

Milk, full cream	11 cups / 2 lt
Sugar	1 cup / 150 gm
Pistachios (*pista*), chopped	10
Almonds (*badam*), chopped	10
Vetiver (*kewda*) essence	a few drops
Silver leaves (*varq*)	3-4

Method:

1. Boil the milk in a wok (*kadhai*); add the sugar and cook on low heat, stirring continuously. As the milk simmers a layer of cream will form on the surface. Push this to the side of the wok.
2. Continue pushing the cream on the side till all the milk is converted into cream.
3. Scrape the sides of the wok and scoop out the cream into a serving dish.
4. Add the pistachios and almonds. Sprinkle some vetiver essence and serve garnished with silver leaves. Best served cold.

Note: *This is best served in earthen bowls.*

Phal Mai Rabri Kulfi

Indian ice cream set in apples and oranges

Preparation time: 1 hr.
Cooking time: 1 hr.
Serves: 6

Ingredients:

Milk, full cream	5½ cups / 1 lt
Sugar	1 cup / 150 gm
Saffron (*kesar*), dissolved in 2 tbsp water (see p. 7)	a few strands
Black grapes (*kala angoor*)	10
Green grapes (*hara angoor*)	10
Pistachios (*pista*)	15
Apples (*seb*)	3
Oranges (*santra*)	3

Method:

1. Pour the milk in a thick-bottomed pan, simmer till reduced to half the amount.
2. Add the sugar and cook till it dissolves in the milk. Boil till a semi-solid mass remains.
3. Add the prepared saffron, grapes, and pistachios. Keep aside.
4. Slice off the tops of the apples, remove the core and carefully scoop out the inside portion of the fruit. Keep the shell intact.
5. Cut the top of the orange and remove all the pulp, only the orange shell should remain.
6. Fill the orange and apple cups with the milk mixture. (Traditionally a small earthenware disc is used to cover, then sealed with wheat dough.) Chill the stuffed fruits in an earthen pot filled with ice for 1 hour or till it sets. Cut in slices and serve.

Suggested Menus

Non-vegetarian

Nahari Gosht (*Spicy lamb in a thick gravy*) 18

Tandoori Murgh (*Roast chicken*) 26

or

Vegetarian

Aloo Ki Khatti Tarkari (*Easy-to-make potato dish*) 38

Dum Karela (*Bitter gourd cooked on a slow fire*) 42

Accompaniments

Bharvin Puri (*Black gram-stuffed fried bread)* 54

Cholia Pulao (*Horse gram rice*) 69

Pudina Chutney (*Mint chutney*) 75

Dessert

Gajar Halwa (*Saffron-flavoured carrot pudding*) 84

Non-vegetarian

Khara Masala Gosht (*Lamb cooked with whole spices*) 22

Machchi Methi (*Fish flavoured with fenugreek)* 33

or

Vegetarian

Sarson Ka Saag (*Spicy mustard greens*) 44

Dal Makhani (*Rich and creamy black gram*) 52

Accompaniments

Makkai Ki Roti (*Maize flour bread*) 63

Yakhni Pulao (*Rice with lamb stew*) 70

Nimbu Ka Achar (*Lemon pickle*) 72

Dessert

Phirni (*Powdered rice pudding*) 88

Glossary of Cooking Terms

Dum — Slow oven or *dum pukht* cooking means cooking on a very low flame in a vessel with a tightly-fitted lid, which is sometimes sealed with dough or aluminium foil. Heat is applied from above and below the pot so that the food stews slowly in its own juices, and absorbs the delicate flavours of the added spices and herbs.

Marinade — To soak meat, fish or vegetable in a mixture of seasoning ingredients to add flavour and to make it tender.

Purée — To press food through a fine sieve or blend it in a blender or food processor to a smooth, thick mixture.

Steam — Cook by heat or steam. Generally food to be steamed is put in a perforated container and placed above a pan of boiling water. The food should not come into contact with the water.

Tandoor — *Tandoor* is a large coal-fired oven. It is easily adaptable to the oven, the electrical grill or the microwave. *Tandoori* is akin to the western barbecue, but with more delicate flavours and with marinades which enhance the flavour of the principle ingredient.

Temper — To fry spices and flavourings in hot oil or ghee, and to pour this over the main preparation.

Index

ACCOMPANIMENTS

Breads

Rice

Chutneys and Pickles

DESSERTS

ISBN: 978-81-7436-196-7

Fourth impression
Published in India by Roli Books
in arrangement with Roli & Janssen BV
M-75, Greater Kailash II (Market), New Delhi-110 048, India
Tel.: ++91-11-40682000, Fax: ++91-11-29217185
E-mail: info@rolibooks.com, Website: www.rolibooks.com

Photographs: Sunny Singh

Printed and bound in Singapore